WEIGHT TRAINING WORKOUTS that WORK

-VOLUME II-

JAMES ORVIS

Ideal Publishing
www.weighttrainingworkouts.com

Note to Readers:
The information in this book is intended to provide a safe, effective
weight training program. Before starting this or any exercise program,
please consult with your health care provider. The author and publisher
are not responsible for any outcomes.

Weight Training Workouts that Work: Volume II

Published by:
Ideal Publishing
33806 Pine View Lane
Crosslake, MN 56442

Email: james@weighttrainingworkouts.com
Website: www.weighttrainingworkouts.com

ISBN: 0-9675188-3-0

Editing: Kay Johnson
Cover Design: Kelley Stafne

Printed in the United States of America

First Printing: January 2004

Library of Congress Control Number: 2003106611

This book is dedicated to my father.
The best man I have ever known.

Contents

Part I: 12 Weeks to a New You

Contents

Part II: The Best Weight Training Exercises

Contents

Part II: The Best Weight Training Exercises

Contents

Part II: The Best Weight Training Exercises

People are always blaming their circumstances for what they are. I don't believe in circumstances. The people who get on in this world are the people who get up and look for the circumstances they want, and, if they can't find them, make them.

- George Bernard Shaw

Introduction

**Weight training is essential to losing weight,
keeping it off and looking your best.
Period!**

**A great workout program is needed
for maximum results.
Period!**

Muscle is your engine. It burns close to 90% of your calories everyday. Because most of us are "clerks" in this day and age, we don't perform a lot of physical activity like cutting down trees or plowing the fields like our ancestors. Consequently, we are losing muscle because our bodies do not need it anymore. We are burning fewer calories and gaining fat!

A great workout program will add muscle fast!

Every new pound of muscle you add burns 60 extra calories a day. Just think...If you add 10 pounds of lean muscle tissue on this 12 week program (which is very possible), you will be using 600 more calories a day.

You turn into a fat burning machine 24 hours a day!

Weight training is the best way to *make* your body gain back its lean muscle. Weight training should be quick, simple and fun. This proven 12 week plan will reshape your body with new lean muscle tissue and fat loss.

Volume II is the workout program that works!

Introduction

Weight Training Workouts that Work: Volume II

- 12-week plan. You will see major changes in your body *and* health in 12 weeks. Try to follow the workouts as closely as possible for maximum results in the shortest time possible.

- Follow these proven workouts and keep track of your progress. Your strength will increase, you energy will jump and your body fat will plummet.

- The best weight training exercises with simple instructions and three detailed photos of each exercise. Make sure you perform the exercises correctly for utmost safety, fat loss and lean muscle gains.

- Easy to use. Take this book to your workouts and follow the routines. The exercises are at your fingertips for a reference at all times. It's that clearcut for creating the body you have always wanted. Get started today!

- *If you have limited or no weight training experience, I highly recommend starting with **Weight Training Workouts that Work**. After you complete the 12-week program then proceed to Volume II.*

Just trust yourself,
then you will know
how to live.

- Goethe

The Four Keys to Weight Training Success

There are many factors to successful weight training. After you plod through all the facts and opinions of the many, there are four main principles you must know. Using this wisdom will guarantee the best results with weight training.

1. Proper Form

The exercises you will perform are described with simple instructions and pictures. Study and practice the exercises with light weights until you become comfortable with the movements. Your form is crucial for maximum results and safety. Follow the exercise technique section as closely as possible. Do not watch other people workout, most are doing it wrong.

2. Intensity

Once you learn proper exercise form, you should put total concentration into every rep of each set. Focus on the muscles you are working. Study and practice the exercises, so you know which muscles are being used. Weight training is at least 50 percent mental. Learn to concentrate on the muscles you are working, and they will become lean and fat free!

The second part to intensity, and this is very, very important. Do as many repetitions as you can, and then try 2 more, always with good form, of course. *This is called muscle fatigue or muscle failure.* The main reason your body is going to change (lose fat, firm up, add muscle, become stronger and healthier), is because your body believes it has to in order to survive. It is that simple. **If you do not challenge your body by trying a couple more reps, it will stay the same.** These are called the magic reps. They truly are because they will give you a fit and fabulous body everyone will be talking about.

6

The Four Keys to Weight Training Success

3. Variety

The third principle you must know is variety. Your body needs to be challenged, as in muscle fatigue, but it also is super-adaptable. If you do the same workout, day after day, week after week, you will get diminishing returns with every workout. Little to no results! Even if you are giving your best effort this will happen. Your body learns very quickly the exercises, weights used, reps, and sets. Because it adapts it will use less muscle to perform the exercises. This is exactly what you do not want to happen. You want to keep your body guessing, so it is constantly changing and improving.

4. Consistency

The last principle to successful weight training is that your body needs regular weight training exercise to make improvements in your health and physical appearance. This does not mean you need to workout for hours every day. This is exactly what you do not want to do. Like many people who start an exercise program, you will most likely wear out your body and quit. Consistency means following this book as closely as possible. The proven routines will give you maximum results with a commitment of only an hour or two per week. That's not much time to invest in your health and body. It will be one of the best investments you ever make!

Getting Started
What you really need to know!

Barbell (BB)
Long bar usually 4 to 7 feet in length, you hold it with both hands.

Dumbbell (DB)
Short bars about a foot in length, you can hold one in each hand. Dumbbells come in a variety of designs and sizes.

Repetition (Rep)
Lifting the weight and lowering the weight to the starting point equals one repetition.

Set
Completing as many repetitions as you can on an exercise equals one set.

Tempo
The speed that you perform the exercise.

Lift the weight for 1-2 seconds.
This is called the *positive* part of the exercise

Lower the weight for 2-3 seconds.
This is called the *negative* part of the exercise

A slow, controlled tempo makes your muscles do all the work. A controlled speed is also easier on your joints.

Breathing
Proper breathing is very important and you need to practice and exaggerate your breathing when you first start weight training. *Do not hold your breath!*

Exhale when you lift (*positive part*) the weight.
Inhale when you lower (*negative part*) the weight.

8

Getting Started
What you really need to know!

Warming up

Always warm-up before weight training. The best way to warm up is to do approximately five to 10 minutes of a cardiovascular activity. Walking, biking or the stair climber all will work nicely. Second, lift light weights, using about 50 percent of the weight you will be using during your workout routine. Warm up on all the exercises you are going to perform during your workout. To function properly, your muscles need the increased blood flow that a warm-up provides. Most people do not warm-up enough. Make sure you do!

When you are ready to give *maximum effort*, begin your workout.

Amount of weight to use on each exercise

Each exercise has a range of weight to choose from in pounds.

The weight is recommended for females.
Men should double the recommended weight.

Always start with the lightest weight suggested!

When the weight is recommended for a dumbbell (DB) exercise, the weight is for each dumbbell.

These are only recommended weights, so you will know where to begin on each exercise if you are new to weight training or a particular exercise.

Make sure to increase the weight when it is too light!!

Getting Started
What you really need to know!

Muscle Fibers
Your body is composed of many different kinds of muscle fibers. There are two main types we are concerned within this book.

1. Endurance Muscle Fibers
   They increase in endurance but do not gain much in size or strength. This increase will <u>not</u> assist a lot in burning more calories and fat at rest. Endurance muscles respond best to aerobic activity and high repetition weight training (more than 20 reps).

2. Strength Muscle Fibers
   They become stronger, larger and more abundant with proper weight training. This correlates into more calories burned at rest, even when you are lying on the sofa! These are the muscle fibers you want to target when lifting weights. They respond best to 5-15 repetitions to muscle failure.

Muscle Fatigue (Muscle Failure)
You cannot complete one more rep with good form.

Rest Periods
Amount of time you rest between sets.

Spotter
A spotter helps the lifter during the exercise. He or she assists in moving the weights into the starting position, helps during the lift so more reps are possible and encourages the lifter to give his or her best effort.

If exercise equipment is not available
Choose a different exercise for the same muscle group.

Common sense is not so common.

- Voltaire

10 Secrets to Success

1. **Find a workout partner**. One of the best things you can do to ensure success with your weight training program is to find a reliable workout partner. They will make you show up, push you when you need to be pushed and help you with those extra reps. Finding the right one makes weight training a lot more fun and productive.

2. **Don't watch other people workout.** There are a few people who are weight training correctly but *most* are not doing it right! Stick with the proven exercises and workouts in this book and you will see sensational results before you know it.

3. **Do aerobic activity on off days or after weight training.** For maximum fat loss and muscle gain, do your cardio on your non-lifting days if time permits. This will give your muscles time to recover from weight training and become stronger. If you want to do your cardio on your weight training day, do it *after* lifting weights. Weight training uses a lot of quick energy, the sugar in your body called glucose and glycogen. After your weight training workout, your body is low on "sugar" and has to use fat for energy. This is what you want to happen when performing your aerobic activity. Do cardio 2-4x per week, 20-30 minutes per session. *Make it an activity that you enjoy so you will do it consistently!*

4. **Stretch at the end of your workouts.** <u>Do not</u> stretch at the beginning of you workouts (but always warm up thoroughly with aerobic activity <u>and</u> light weight training). Your muscles need to be warmed up and elastic to stretch safely. You want to stretch during and after lifting weights. A great book on stretching is *The New Power Program* by Dr. Michael Colgan.

5. **Workout at the same time everyday.** Have a set schedule for your weight training workouts. If you don't something will always come up to prevent you from making it to your workout. You have to make it a priority in your life or there will be too many distractions. Schedule your workout for the same time everyday and keep it as best as possible. Your body will thank you!

10 Secrets to Success

6. **Try working out for 10 minutes.** Some days you will not feel like exercising. What do you do? Go to your workout, try it for 10 minutes and see how you feel. 99 percent of the time you will feel so amazing that you will finish your workout and make big-time improvements on your body!

7. **Make every workout a little better than your last one.** Every workout should be a challenge to you. Trying one more rep, increasing the weight, or using better form. It's you and only you that is going to make a body that you have always dreamed of having. *"Just do it"* as the saying goes!

8. **Don't count reps until you are tired.** You want your muscles to fatigue close to the prescribed number of repetitions laid out in this book. BUT you do not want to make that number all important. It is a reference. Far too many people are only concerned with completing a certain number of reps. **Your muscles do not count, they respond to a stress.** If you are suppose to do 10 reps and get to 10 reps and can still do more with good form – do them! You can increase the weight on your next set or workout. Start counting when your muscles become tired. Tell yourself you are going to do 3 more reps. This is when your body really firms up and turns into a fat burning machine!

10 Secrets to Success

9. **Change your rep speed.** As you have read previously, variety is one of the big keys to consistent results. A fantastic way to keep your body improving, *especially if you have been weight training for over a year*, is to change your rep speed. Instead of always doing the same rep speed – lowering the weight for 2-3 seconds, lifting the weight for 1-2 seconds – try a different tempo. Here are some examples.

1) Lower the weight for 2 seconds
   Pause at the bottom for a second
   Lift the weight for 2 seconds

2) Lower the weight for 2 seconds
   No Pause at the bottom
   Explode on the lift
   (lift as fast as you can but always under control!)

3) Lower the weight for 5 seconds
   Pause at the bottom for 2 seconds
   Lift the weight for 2 seconds

   Try the different tempos for a few workouts
   and find the one that works best for you.

10. **Stop if you are fatigued.** The last secret is a little vague. If and only if you have physically given everything you have during your workout and have not finished, but are exhausted – stop. It is better to cut your workout short when you body tells you to, than to keep going. You can only make so much progress in one workout and if you have lifted hard, some days you are wiped out after a few great sets. Go home and let your muscles grow! However, this does not give you a license to stop your workout anytime you are feeling a little fatigued. Only stop the workout short when your body is exhausted, not your brain telling you to hit the showers. You will know the difference after lifting weights a short time.

14

NOTICE

This is an exceptional weight training program from the post-beginner all the way to the advanced lifter.

<u>BUT there is not one workout that fits everyone</u>. I have intentionally left out exercises that target certain body parts that some people may not want to over develop.

TRAPEZOIDS
FOREARMS
NECK

If you wish to promote these bodyparts, use exercises that will target the muscles and <u>add them to the workouts.</u>

Do or do not.
There is no try.

- Yoda

Week 1: Giant Sets

Giant sets are a fabulous way to fatigue your muscles so your body will become shapelier and tighter. You will do 3 different exercises in succession with no rest. Works with opposing muscles or the same muscle groups.

Example: *Leg Curl to Leg Extensions to Leg Press*

Giant Sets are a proven method that will make the muscles work harder than normal, so you can get closer to muscle failure (exactly what you want to happen in muscle building). When the muscle fails, you will not be able to lift the weight for any more repetitions. Then it will become stronger, firmer and more numerous.

Your body will turn into a firm, fat-burning machine!

Remember to warm-up thoroughly before starting your workout. This is very important and most people start lifting too hard before their bodies are ready. Safety first – injuries can last forever! When you warm-up properly your muscles *and* mind are ready to give maximum effort.

Let's get started on your new body!

Week 1: Giant Sets

Week 1

- Three workouts.
- Non consecutive days. Example: Monday-Wednesday-Friday or whatever works for you. Try to have at least one day of rest between weight training workouts. You can do cardio on the non-lifting days. This works great for increased fat loss!
- Two sets per exercise.
- 8-12 repetitions to muscle fatigue. Each exercise will have a prescribed number of reps for the best results. Try to hit muscle fatigue at or around this number. Start with the lightest weight recommended and add more weight if it is too easy and you are completing more reps than suggested to muscular fatigue.
- Remember - men <u>double</u> the recommended weight.
- No rest during the Giant Set. Go as quickly as possible between the 3 exercises. Try to have the exercises in close proximity of each other. *Sometimes it is difficult at a busy health club. Do the best you can or substitute an exercise that is available and works the same muscles.*
- Rest 2-3 minutes before starting your next Giant Set.
- Total body workouts.

Week 1: Giant Sets
Workout 1
-Total Body-

Exercise	Your Goal		Your Set	
	Reps x	Weight	Reps x	Weight
1. Walking Lunges	15	0-15		
Leg Press	15	50-150		
Calf Raise*	15	50-150		
2. Walking Lunges	15	0-15		
Leg Press	15	50-150		
Calf Raise*	15	50-150		
3. Lat Pulldown**	10	50-75		
Bench Press	10	25-50		
DB Press	10	8-20		
4. Lat Pulldown**	10	50-75		
Bench Press	10	25-50		
DB Press	10	8-20		
5. Lat Pulldown**	10	50-75		
Bench Press	10	25-50		
DB Press	10	8-20		

*Do Calf Raises on the Leg Press or any Calf Machine
**Use the Triangle Bar

Week 1: Giant Sets
Workout 2
-Total Body-

Exercise	Your Goal		Your Set	
	Reps x	Weight	Reps x	Weight
1. Rev. Crunches	F*	0		
Ab Bench Crunch	F	0		
Rev. Crunches	F	0		
2. Rev. Crunches	F	0		
Ab Bench Crunch	F	0		
Rev. Crunches	F	0		
3. Hammer Curls	12	8-20		
2 DB Pullovers	12	5-15		
Cable Curls	12	15-30		
4. Hammer Curls	12	8-20		
2 DB Pullovers	12	5-15		
Cable Curls	12	15-30		
5. DB Squats	10	10-20		
Leg Curls	10	40-70		
Deadlifts	10	10-45		
6. DB Squats	10	10-20		
Leg Curls	10	40-70		
Deadlifts	10	10-45		

*F= Muscle fatigue. You can't complete any more reps with good form.

20

Week 1: Giant Sets
Workout 3
-Total Body-

Exercise	Your Goal		Your Set	
	Reps	x Weight	Reps	x Weight
1. Ball Crunches	8	8-20		
Pushdowns	8	20-40		
Kickbacks	8	5-15		
2. Ball Crunches	8	8-20		
Pushdowns	8	20-40		
Kickbacks	8	5-15		
3. Ball Crunches	8	8-20		
Pushdowns	8	20-40		
Kickbacks	8	5-15		
4. BB Squats	12	45-75		
Leg Extensions	12	20-50		
Leg Curls	12	30-60		
5. BB Squats	12	45-75		
Leg Extensions	12	20-50		
Leg Curls	12	30-60		
6. BB Squats	12	45-75		
Leg Extensions	12	20-50		
Leg Curls	12	30-60		

Week 2: Giant Sets

How was week 1? Good workouts or great workouts?

Did your muscles feel sore and tight the day after working out? They should! This is called *delayed onset muscle soreness* or DOMS. When you are lifting with good form and pushing yourself on the last couple of hard reps, your muscles actually get small micro-tears in them because they are not used to muscle failure. This is a good thing. Your body then must repair these muscles, which takes a lot of calories, so they will be able to perform this exercise next time. This is how you add muscle, become stronger, leaner and more fit. Pretty simple concept! Best of all, it's a fact and it always works.

If your muscles are never sore or you do not feel tired right after weight training and tight the following day – it is time to turn up the intensity. Once you become used to the feeling of doing every set the best you can, you will love it. As I have said many times before, it is more productive to do one set to muscle failure than to do 20 easy sets. Your body will change more from the failure set, because it has to adapt to survive.*

Week 2

- Three workouts. Non-consecutive days.
- Giant Sets. No rest between exercises.
- Rest 2-3 minutes before starting your next Giant Set.
- Split routines. You will do different muscle groups at each workout. This allows the muscle you just worked to rest, recover and become stronger.

If you are new to weight training or have not lifted weights recently, I highly recommend starting with the first book, Weight Training Workouts that Work.

Trust yourself.
Think for yourself.
Act for yourself.
Speak for yourself.
Be yourself.
Imitation is suicide.

- Marva Collins

Week 2: Giant Sets
Workout 1
-Back, Biceps-

Exercise	Your Goal		Your Set	
	Reps	x Weight	Reps	x Weight
1. 2 DB Pullovers	10	5-15		
2 DB Rows	10	8-20		
Rear Raise	10	3-15		
2. 2 DB Pullovers	10	5-15		
2 DB Rows	10	8-20		
Rear Raise	10	3-15		
3. Lat Pulldown*	10	40-70		
Pullovers	10	10-25		
Lat Pulldown**	10	40-70		
4. Lat Pulldown*	10	40-70		
Pullovers	10	10-25		
Lat Pulldown**	10	40-70		
5. Incline Curls	12	8-15		
DB Curls	12	10-20		
BB Curls	12	25-50		
6. Incline Curls	12	8-15		
DB Curls	12	10-20		
BB Curls	12	25-50		

*Wide Grip
**Underhand Grip

Week 2: Giant Sets
Workout 2
-Lower Body-

Exercise	Your Goal		Your Set	
	Reps x	Weight	Reps x	Weight
1. Walking Lunges	F	5-15		
Deadlifts	15	20-60		
Walking Lunges	F	5-15		
2. Walking Lunges	F	5-15		
Deadlifts	15	20-60		
Walking Lunges	F	5-15		
3. Calf Raises	20	50-100		
Leg Curls	10	30-60		
Calf Raises	20	50-100		
4. Calf Raises	20	50-100		
Leg Curls	10	30-60		
Calf Raises	20	50-100		
5. Ball V-Ups	F	0		
Ball Crunches	F	0		
Crunches	F	0		

F=Muscle Fatigue

Week 2: Giant Sets
Workout 3
-Chest, Shoulders, Triceps-

Exercise	Your Goal		Your Set	
	Reps x	Weight	Reps x	Weight
1. Incline Flys	8	10-20		
Incline DB Bench	8	8-15		
SkullKrushers	8	5-15		
2. Incline Flys	8	10-20		
Incline DB Bench	8	8-15		
SkullKrushers	8	5-15		
3. Front Raise	12	3-10		
BB Press	12	15-30		
Side Raise	12	5-12		
4. Front Raise	12	3-10		
BB Press	12	15-30		
Side Raise	12	5-12		
5. Overhead Ext.	15	10-20		
Pushdowns	15	20-40		
Kickbacks	15	3-10		
6. Overhead Ext.	15	10-20		
Pushdowns	15	20-40		
Kickbacks	15	3-10		

*It is common sense to
take a method and try it.
If it fails, admit it frankly
and try another.
But above all,
try something.*

- **Franklin D. Roosevelt**

Week 3: 1 Muscle a Day

Now it's time to start having some serious fun! You are going to weight train for five consecutive days in week 3. The workouts are going to be short and intense with an added twist for more results.

Most of your workouts should be 45 minutes or less. If you are weight training longer than this, (don't count your warm-up and stretching), you could be over-training. When you surpass the 45 minute mark of quality weight training, your testosterone drops dramatically (yes, ladies, you have testosterone too). With lowered testosterone you have hit the wall, as they say, and are not going to make any more progress that day. In fact you will probably "fatigue" your muscle too much and it will take a long time for your muscle to recover and become stronger. If you constantly do this, especially the older you get, you will over-train. This is when bad things happen - injuries, no results, strength loss, fatigue, insomnia, always tired, loss of sex drive, and lethargy.

Rule of thumb – keep your weight training workouts under an hour and intense for maximum results.

Here's the added twist for week 3. You will be incorporating *partials*. Partials are another way to add intensity and variety to your workouts, so you will keep building lean muscle and burning fat. Partials (also called ¼ reps) will be done at the end of a set to extend it. After you can't do any more reps with good form, you will continue with the same weight but do 5 partial reps, shortening the range of motion to ¼ of the rep range.

Week 3: 1 Muscle a Day

Partials can be done anywhere in an exercise's range of motion. <u>You will be using it on the top part of the lift.</u> When you start the lowering (negative) part of the exercise, lower only ¼ and immediately push up hard on the positive part of the lift. You will be comfortable with partials after a little practice!

You will really feel your muscles working because partials take the muscles past what they normally can do. You will hit a higher level of muscular failure. Because this is high intensity and can lead to over-training if overused, you will only use this on the last set of each exercise.

Partials Example: Bench Press

START

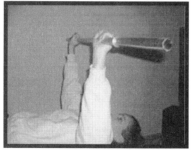

FINISH

Week 3

- Five workouts on consecutive days.
- 1 bodypart per workout.
- Straight sets. Rest 2 minutes between sets.
- 3 sets per exercise.
- Partials on last set (3rd set) of each exercise.
- Go to muscle failure on each set.
- Use a spotter if available!

Week 3: 1 Muscle a Day
Workout 1
-Back-

Exercise	Your Goal		Your Set	
	Reps	x Weight	Reps	x Weight
1. Lat Pulldown*	8	40-70		
Lat Pulldown	8	40-70		
Lat Pulldown**	8	40-70		
2. Rear Raise	8	3-15		
Rear Raise	8	3-15		
Rear Raise**	8	3-15		
3. Pullovers	8	10-25		
Pullovers	8	10-25		
Pullovers**	8	10-25		
4. 2 DB Rows	8	10-20		
2 DB Rows	8	10-20		
2 DB Rows **	8	10-20		

*Underhand Grip
**Do 5 partial reps when you can't complete any more full reps

Week 3: 1 Muscle a Day
Workout 2
-Legs-

Exercise	Your Goal		Your Set	
	Reps x	Weight	Reps x	Weight
1. Calf Raises	15	75-150		
Calf Raises	15	75-150		
Calf Raises*	15	75-150		
2. Leg Press	8	75-150		
Leg Press	8	75-150		
Leg Press*	8	75-150		
3. DB Squats	8	10-25		
DB Squats	8	10-25		
DB Squats*	8	10-25		
4. BB Squats	8	30-60		
BB Squats	8	30-60		
BB Squats*	8	30-60		

*Do 5 partial reps when you can't complete any more full reps

Week 3: 1 Muscle a Day
Workout 3
-Abs-

Exercise	Your Goal		Your Set	
	Reps x	Weight	Reps x	Weight
1. Ab Bench Crunch	15	0-15		
Ab Bench Crunch	15	0-15		
Ab Bench Crunch*	15	0-15		
2. Rev. Crunches	8	0		
Rev. Crunches	8	0		
Rev Crunches**	8	0		
3. Ball Crunches	8	0		
Ball Crunches	8	0		
Ball Crunches*	8	0		
4. Wood Chop(R)**	8	15-30		
Wood Chop(L)**	8	15-30		

*Do 5 partial reps when you can't complete any more full reps
**No Partials

Week 3: 1 Muscle a Day
Workout 4
-Chest-

Exercise	Your Goal		Your Set	
	Reps x	Weight	Reps x	Weight
1. DB Bench Press	8	10-25		
DB Bench Press	8	10-25		
DB Bench Press*	8	10-25		
3. Incline DB Bench	8	8-20		
Incline DB Bench	8	8-20		
Incline DB Bench*	8	8-20		
3. BB Bench Press	8	35-70		
BB Bench Press	8	35-70		
BB Bench Press*	8	35-70		
4. Incline Flys	15	5-15		
Incline Flys	15	5-15		
Incline Flys*	15	5-15		

*Do 5 partial reps when you can't complete any more full reps

Week 3: 1 Muscle a Day
Workout 5
-Biceps-

Exercise	Your Goal		Your Set	
	Reps x	Weight	Reps x	Weight
1. Hammer Curls	15	10-25		
Hammer Curls	15	10-25		
Hammer Curls*	15	10-25		
2. Cable Curls	15	20-40		
Cable Curls	15	20-40		
Cable Curls*	15	20-40		
3. Incline Curls	15	8-20		
Incline Curls	15	8-20		
Incline Curls*	15	8-20		
4. BB Curls	15	20-40		
BB Curls	15	20-40		
BB Curls*	15	20-40		

*Do 5 partial reps when you can't complete any more full reps

It's kind of fun to do the impossible.

- **Walt Disney**

Are the partials working? Can you squeeze out 5 partial reps on your last set of each exercise?

If you can't complete 5 partials at the end of the set with good form, try stopping one full repetition sooner this week so you can eke out those 5 heart-pounding, muscle-building partial reps.

If the 5 partials are too easy and you could complete more, make sure you only stop doing full reps when you have hit muscle failure. Then you can start your 5 magic partials!

Using 2 weeks of partials will push you beyond any plateau you might have encountered. It gives your body a whole new muscle fatigue sensation that it has not had before, so it will have to get better at completing this task.

Gain new muscle and lose fat!

Week 4

- Five workouts on consecutive days.
- 1 bodypart per workout.
- Straight sets. Rest 2 minutes between sets.
- 3 sets per exercise.
- Partials on last set (3rd set) of each exercise.
- Go to muscle failure on each set.
- Use a spotter if available!

Everyday,
in every way,
I'm getting better,
and better.

- Emile Cove

Week 4: 1 Muscle a Day
Workout 1
-Shoulders-

Exercise	Your Goal		Your Set	
	Reps x	Weight	Reps x	Weight
1. BB Press	10	15-30		
BB Press	10	15-30		
BB Press*	10	15-30		
2. Front Raise	10	5-10		
Front Raise	10	5-10		
Front Raise*	10	5-10		
3. DB Press	10	8-15		
DB Press	10	8-15		
DB Press*	10	8-15		
4. Side Raise	10	5-10		
Side Raise	10	5-10		
Side Raise*	10	5-10		

*Do 5 partial reps when you can't complete any more full reps

Week 4: 1 Muscle a Day
Workout 2
-Legs-

Exercise	Your Goal		Your Set	
	Reps	x Weight	Reps	x Weight
1. Deadlifts	15	25-50		
Deadlifts	15	25-50		
Deadlifts**	15	25-50		
2. Walking Lunges	F	5-15		
Walking Lunges	F	5-15		
Walking Lunges**	F	5-15		
3. Leg Extensions	15	25-50		
Leg Extensions	15	25-50		
Leg Extensions*	15	25-50		
4. Leg Curls	8	30-60		
Leg Curls	8	30-60		
Leg Curls*	8	30-60		

*Do 5 partial reps when you can't complete any more full reps
**Do <u>not</u> do partials

Week 4: 1 Muscle a Day
Workout 3
-Abs-

Exercise	Your Goal Reps	x	Weight	Your Set Reps	x	Weight
1. Crunches	15		0			
Crunches	15		0			
Crunches*	15		0			
2. Ball V-Ups	15		0			
Ball V-Ups	15		0			
Ball V-Ups*	15		0			
3. Wood Chop (R)	15		15-30			
Wood Chop (R)	15		15-30			
4. Wood Chop (L)	15		15-30			
Wood Chop (L)	15		15-30			

*Do 5 partial reps when you can't complete any more full reps
No partials on the Wood Chop

Week 4: 1 Muscle a Day
Workout 4
-Triceps-

Exercise	Your Goal		Your Set	
	Reps	x Weight	Reps	x Weight
1. Overhead Ext.	12	10-25		
Overhead Ext.	12	10-25		
Overhead Ext.*	12	10-25		
2. SkullKrushers	12	8-15		
SkullKrushers	12	8-15		
SkullKrushers*	12	8-15		
3. Pushdowns	12	15-30		
Pushdowns	12	15-30		
Pushdowns*	12	15-30		
4. Kickbacks	12	5-10		
Kickbacks	12	5-10		
Kickbacks*	12	5-10		

*Do 5 partial reps when you can't complete any more full reps

Week 4: 1 Muscle a Day
Workout 5
-Back-

Exercise	Your Goal		Your Set	
	Reps	x Weight	Reps	x Weight
1. Pullovers	8	15-30		
Pullovers	8	15-30		
Pullovers*	8	15-30		
2. Lat Pulldowns**	8	40-70		
Lat Pulldowns	8	40-70		
Lat Pulldowns*	8	40-70		
3. 2 DB Rows	8	15-25		
2 DB Rows	8	15-25		
2 DB Rows*	8	15-25		
4. Rear Raise	8	5-10		
Rear Raise	8	5-10		
Rear Raise*	8	5-10		

*Do 5 partial reps when you can't complete any more full reps
**Use Triangle Bar

Week 5: Big 3

Getting stronger will help you in building a healthy, fit body.

Stronger bones-
Stronger tendons -
Stronger ligaments-
Stronger joints-
Stronger muscles-

Then You Will Be Able To Lift Heavier Weights....Easier!

The best way to become stronger is to do big compound exercises for low reps. Compound exercises work a lot of the big muscles at the same time. Some of the best are Squats, Leg Press, Deadlifts, Bench Presses, Lat Pulldowns and Pullovers.

Low reps are 5-8 repetitions to failure. (Doing less than 5 reps to failure might yield more relative strength gains but can be very dangerous without a competent spotter, perfect form and ample experience. It is also very hard on your joints.) When you complete 5-8 reps, this will target what are called type IIb muscle fibers. These fast twitched muscle fibers can become stronger and bigger in a very short time with a proven workout.

The "Big 3" is a legendary way to rapidly build up your strength and muscle size. This workout consists of 1 pushing exercise, 1 pulling exercise and 1 lower body exercise. You complete five sets of each exercise for 5-8 reps, resting 3-5 minutes between sets.

Week 5: Big 3

Example

Barbell Bench Press
Set 1: 100lbs x 8 reps – rest 3-5 minutes
Set 2: 100lbs x 8 reps – rest 3-5 minutes
Set 3: 100lbs x 8 reps – rest 3-5 minutes
Set 4: 100lbs x 8 reps – rest 3-5 minutes
Set 5: 100lbs x 8 reps – rest 3-5 minutes

Lat Pulldown
Set 1: 90lbs x 8 reps – rest 3-5 minutes
Set 2: 90lbs x 8 reps – rest 3-5 minutes
Set 3: 90lbs x 8 reps – rest 3-5 minutes
Set 4: 90lbs x 8 reps – rest 3-5 minutes
Set 5: 90lbs x 8 reps – rest 3-5 minutes

Barbell Squats
Set 1: 150lbs x 8 reps – rest 3-5 minutes
Set 2: 150lbs x 8 reps – rest 3-5 minutes
Set 3: 150lbs x 8 reps – rest 3-5 minutes
Set 4: 150lbs x 8 reps – rest 3-5 minutes
Set 5: 150lbs x 8 reps – rest 3-5 minutes

You want to rest at least 3 minutes between sets. This allows enough time for your body and muscles to recover, so you have maximum strength again.

Week 6

- Three workouts.
- Non-consecutive days.
- Total body workouts.
- 1 pushing exercise
- 1 pulling exercise
- 1 lower body exercise
- 5 sets per exercise
- 5 or 8 reps to muscle failure.
- Rest 3-5 minutes between sets.
- Use a spotter!!
- *Make sure you warm-up thoroughly before starting this workout. You are using HEAVY WEIGHTS and your muscles need to be ready to exert maximum effort safely!*

*The secret of success
is to know something
nobody else knows.*

- Aristotle Onassis

Week 5: Big Three
Workout 1
-Total Body-

Exercise	Your Goal		Your Set	
	Reps	x Weight	Reps	x Weight
1. BB Bench Press	8	45-90		
BB Bench Press	8	45-90		
BB Bench Press	8	45-90		
BB Bench Press	8	45-90		
BB Bench Press	8	45-90		
2. BB Squats	8	45-80		
BB Squats	8	45-80		
BB Squats	8	45-80		
BB Squats	8	45-80		
BB Squats	8	45-80		
3. Lat Pulldown*	8	50-80		
Lat Pulldown	8	50-80		
Lat Pulldown	8	50-80		
Lat Pulldown	8	50-80		
Lat Pulldown	8	50-80		

* Use Wide Grip

Week 5: Big Three
Workout 2
-Total Body-

Exercise	Your Goal		Your Set	
	Reps x	Weight	Reps x	Weight
1. Deadlifts	8	35-70		
Deadlifts	8	35-70		
Deadlifts	8	35-70		
Deadlifts	8	35-70		
Deadlifts	8	35-70		
2. Leg Press	8	100-200		
Leg Press	8	100-200		
Leg Press	8	100-200		
Leg Press	8	100-200		
Leg Press	8	100-200		
3. Incline DB Bench	8	30-60		
Incline DB Bench	8	30-60		
Incline DB Bench	8	30-60		
Incline DB Bench	8	30-60		
Incline DB Bench	8	30-60		

Week 5: Big Three
Workout 3
-Total Body-

Exercise	Your Goal Reps x Weight		Your Set Reps x Weight	
1. DB Squats	8	15-30		
DB Squats	8	15-30		
DB Squats	8	15-30		
DB Squats	8	15-30		
DB Squats	8	15-30		
2. DB Bench Press	8	15-30		
DB Bench Press	8	15-30		
DB Bench Press	8	15-30		
DB Bench Press	8	15-30		
DB Bench Press	8	15-30		
3. Pullovers	8	30-60		
Pullovers	8	30-60		
Pullovers	8	30-60		
Pullovers	8	30-60		
Pullovers	8	30-60		

Week 6: Big Three

Did you feel the difference with week five workouts compared to the first four weeks? When you lift heavy weights for low reps it feels much different than medium weights.

1. The first rep feels *really* heavy.
2. You don't feel that burning sensation at the end of the set.
3. Your muscles don't have that tired, fatigued feeling.
4. You are not out of breath.

Sometimes it feels like you are not working out hard enough. You are! Occasionally you need to increase your absolute strength to make all your other workouts more productive. When you are stronger, you will lift heavier weights or be able to do another rep or two at the end of the set. These are the "magic reps" that will change your body forever!

You don't want to lift heavy weight for low reps all the time. This is what power lifters do and they do not have the best bodies ever built and their injuries are frequent. But a two-week cycle every 3 months works miracles in becoming stronger.

Week 6: Big Three

Week 6

- Three workouts.
- Non-consecutive days.
- Total body workouts.
- 1 pushing exercise.
- 1 pulling exercise.
- 1 lower body exercise.
- 5 sets per exercise.
- 5 or 8 reps to muscle failure.
- Rest 3-5 minutes between sets.
- Use a spotter!
- *Make sure you warm-up thoroughly before starting your workout. You are using HEAVY WEIGHTS and your muscles need to be ready to exert maximum effort safely!*

Week 6: Big Three
Workout 1
-Total Body-

Exercise	Your Goal Reps x Weight		Your Set Reps x Weight	
1. Leg Press	5	100-200		
Leg Press	5	100-200		
Leg Press	5	100-200		
Leg Press	5	100-200		
Leg Press	5	100-200		
2. Deadlifts	5	35-70		
Deadlifts	5	35-70		
Deadlifts	5	35-70		
Deadlifts	5	35-70		
Deadlifts	5	35-70		
3. BB Bench Press	5	40-80		
BB Bench Press	5	40-80		
BB Bench Press	5	40-80		
BB Bench Press	5	40-80		
BB Bench Press	5	40-80		

Week 6: Big Three
Workout 2
-Total Body-

Exercise	Your Goal Reps x Weight		Your Set Reps x Weight	
1. Incline DB Bench	5	20-35		
Incline DB Bench	5	20-35		
Incline DB Bench	5	20-35		
Incline DB Bench	5	20-35		
Incline DB Bench	5	20-35		
2. Lat Pulldown*	5	50-80		
Lat Pulldown	5	50-80		
Lat Pulldown	5	50-80		
Lat Pulldown	5	50-80		
Lat Pulldown	5	50-80		
3. BB Squats	5	60-100		
BB Squats	5	60-100		
BB Squats	5	60-100		
BB Squats	5	60-100		
BB Squats	5	60-100		

*Triangle Bar

Week 6: Big Three
Workout 3
-Total Body-

Exercise	Your Goal		Your Set	
	Reps x Weight		Reps x Weight	
1. BB Bench Press	5	40-80		
BB Bench Press	5	40-80		
BB Bench Press	5	40-80		
BB Bench Press	5	40-80		
BB Bench Press	5	40-80		
2. Leg Press	5	125-200		
Leg Press	5	125-200		
Leg Press	5	125-200		
Leg Press	5	125-200		
Leg Press	5	125-200		
3. Deadlifts	8	45-90		
Deadlifts	8	45-90		
Deadlifts	8	45-90		
Deadlifts	8	45-90		
Deadlifts	8	45-90		

Week 7: 12-Minute Workouts

Can you rev-up your metabolism and build muscle in 12 minutes?

ABSOLUTELY!

After doing heavy weights and high volume for 6 weeks, your body needs some recuperation for continuous progress. Quick, high intensity workouts are perfect!

Also, it is mentally gratifying to know you will only be working out for a few minutes. These workouts are easy to get excited about... just rip off a few sets and go home!

Week 7

- Four workouts.
- Split and total body routines.
- Rest only 1 minute between sets.
- Go to failure on every set.
- Remember to warm-up!

Make everything as simple as possible,
but not simpler.

- Albert Einstein

Week 7: 12-Minute Workouts
Workout 1
-Abs-

Exercise	Your Goal Reps x Weight		Your Set Reps x Weight	
1. Rev. Crunches	F	0		
Rev. Crunches	F	0		
2. Wood Chop(R)	10	15-30		
Wood Chop(L)	10	15-30		
Wood Chop(R)	10	15-30		
Wood Chop(L)	10	15-30		
3. Crunches	F	0		
Crunches	F	0		

F= Muscle fatigue
R= Right
L= Left

63

Week 7: 12-Minute Workouts
Workout 2
-Upper Body-

Exercise	Your Goal		Your Set	
	Reps x	Weight	Reps x	Weight
1. BB Press	12	25-50		
BB Press	12	25-50		
2. Overhead Ext.	12	8-20		
Overhead Ext.	12	8-20		
3. 2 DB Rows	12	10-25		
2 DB Rows	12	10-25		
4. Hammer Curls	12	8-20		
Hammer Curls	12	8-20		

Week 7: 12-Minute Workouts
Workout 3
-Total Body-

Exercise	Your Goal		Your Set	
	Reps x	Weight	Reps x	Weight
1. Twisting Bench	10	10-20		
Twisting Bench	10	10-20		
2. Pushdowns	15	20-40		
Pushdowns	15	20-40		
3. Deadlifts	12	30-60		
Deadlifts	12	30-60		
4. Calf Raises	25	75-125		
Calf Raises	25	75-125		

Week 7: 12-Minute Workouts
Workout 4
-Total Body-

Exercise	Your Goal		Your Set	
	Reps x	Weight	Reps x	Weight
1. Rear Raise	10	5-10		
Rear Raise	10	5-10		
Rear Raise	10	5-10		
2. Walking Lunges	F	10-20		
Walking Lunges	F	10-20		
Walking Lunges	F	10-20		
3. Ab Bench Crunch	F	0-20		
Ab Bench Crunch	F	0-20		

F= Muscle Fatigue

Week 8: 12-Minute Workouts

Time for a well deserved break!

You will continue to do 12-Minute Workouts during the eighth week. Your body needs a short break (5-7 days) from all formal exercise including weight training approximately every two months. This allows your muscles *and* all the systems of your body to fully recuperate and re-energize. Without a break from lifting every couple of months, you will become over-trained. This leads to a plateau in results and enthusiasm. You will lift weights only one time this week to avoid over-training. When you come back next week, you will feel energetic and ready to take over the weight room!

Week 8

- 1 workout, <u>beginning of the week</u>.
- Continue 12-Minute Workouts.
- Total body workout.
- Rest 1 minute between sets.
- Go to failure on every set.
- *No organized exercise for the remainder of the week.*
- Rest, grow muscles, get stronger, burn fat, have fun!

He who has begun
has half done.
Dare to be wise;
begin!

- Horace 65-8 B.C.

Week 8: 12-Minute Workouts
Workout 1
-Total Body-

Exercise	Your Goal		Your Set	
	Reps x	Weight	Reps x	Weight
1. DB Squats	10	10-25		
DB Squats	10	10-25		
2. DB Press	10	8-20		
DB Press	10	8-20		
3. Hammer Curls	10	8-20		
Hammer Curls	10	8-20		
4. Ab Bench Crunch	15	0-20		
Ab Bench Crunch	15	0-20		
Ab Bench Crunch	15	0-20		

Attention to health is life's greatest hindrance.

- Plato

Week 9: Volume Training

How was the break? Are you ready to pump some iron and feel your tight muscles again? I bet you're ready to go!

One of the best ways the Eastern Europeans have found to gain new muscle tissue when nothing else works, is *Volume Training*. There are many different versions of this workout, but the method given here is very simple to do and works. Simple but not easy! You will be tired and sore. But after taking a few days off from exercise, Volume Training will be your ticket for packing on muscle and burning fat!

Volume Training

- Same exercise.
- Same weight.
- *Pick a weight where you could complete about 15 reps to failure on your first set.*
- 10 sets.
- 10 reps.
- 1 minute rest between sets.

Example: Bench Press

Set 1 – 10 reps x 100 lbs. Rest 1 Minute.
Set 2 – 10 reps x 100 lbs. Rest 1 Minute.
Set 3 – 10 reps x 100 lbs. Rest 1 Minute.
Set 4 – 10 reps x 100 lbs. Rest 1 Minute.
Set 5 – 10 reps x 100 lbs. Rest 1 Minute.
Set 6 – 10 reps x 100 lbs. Rest 1 Minute.
Set 7 – 10 reps x 100 lbs. Rest 1 Minute.
Set 8 – 10 reps x 100 lbs. Rest 1 Minute.
Set 9 – 10 reps x 100 lbs. Rest 1 Minute.
Set 10- 10 reps x 100 lbs. Rest 1 Minute.

Week 9: Volume Training

Volume Training works perfect with a training partner. By going back and forth, you are resting about a minute between each set when you are spotting each other.

You will find completing all 10 sets can be very taxing, especially when doing big compound exercises like squats. Do the best you can! Complete all 10 sets even if you can't squeeze out 10 reps on every set.

Finding the right amount of weight to use can be difficult in the beginning. Everybody is built different, with some people having more endurance. Experiment – choose a weight where you would hit muscle fatigue around 15 repetitions on your first set. You will find your body responds differently to each exercise. Do the best you can and change the weight next workout if needed.

Week 9

- Three workouts.
- Non-consecutive days.
- Split routines.
- 2 exercises per workout.
- 10 sets per exercise.
- Rest only 1 minute between sets.
- Rest up to 10 minutes before starting the second exercise.

I know of no more
encouraging fact
than the unquestionable
ability of man
to elevate his life
by conscious endeavor.

- **Thoreau**

Week 9: Volume Training
Workout 1
-Chest, Back-

Exercise	Your Goal		Your Set	
	Reps x	Weight	Reps x	Weight
1. Incline DB Bench	10	10-25		
Incline DB Bench	10	10-25		
Incline DB Bench	10	10-25		
Incline DB Bench	10	10-25		
Incline DB Bench	10	10-25		
Incline DB Bench	10	10-25		
Incline DB Bench	10	10-25		
Incline DB Bench	10	10-25		
Incline DB Bench	10	10-25		
Incline DB Bench	10	10-25		
2. Lat Pulldown*	10	40-70		
Lat Pulldown	10	40-70		
Lat Pulldown	10	40-70		
Lat Pulldown	10	40-70		
Lat Pulldown	10	40-70		
Lat Pulldown	10	40-70		
Lat Pulldown	10	40-70		
Lat Pulldown	10	40-70		
Lat Pulldown	10	40-70		
Lat Pulldown	10	40-70		

*Underhand Grip

Week 9: Volume Training
Workout 2
-Legs, Abs-

Exercise	Your Goal Reps x Weight		Your Set Reps x Weight	
1. Leg Press	10	75-125		
Leg Press	10	75-125		
Leg Press	10	75-125		
Leg Press	10	75-125		
Leg Press	10	75-125		
Leg Press	10	75-125		
Leg Press	10	75-125		
Leg Press	10	75-125		
Leg Press	10	75-125		
Leg Press	10	75-125		
2. Ab Bench Crunch	10	0-15		
Ab Bench Crunch	10	0-15		
Ab Bench Crunch	10	0-15		
Ab Bench Crunch	10	0-15		
Ab Bench Crunch	10	0-15		
Ab Bench Crunch	10	0-15		
Ab Bench Crunch	10	0-15		
Ab Bench Crunch	10	0-15		
Ab Bench Crunch	10	0-15		
Ab Bench Crunch	10	0-15		

Week 9: Volume Training
Workout 3
-Arms-

Exercise	Your Goal		Your Set	
	Reps x Weight		Reps x Weight	
1. SkullKrushers	10	8-20		
SkullKrushers	10	8-20		
SkullKrushers	10	8-20		
SkullKrushers	10	8-20		
SkullKrushers	10	8-20		
SkullKrushers	10	8-20		
SkullKrushers	10	8-20		
SkullKrushers	10	8-20		
SkullKrushers	10	8-20		
SkullKrushers	10	8-20		
2. DB Curls	10	8-20		
DB Curls	10	8-20		
DB Curls	10	8-20		
DB Curls	10	8-20		
DB Curls	10	8-20		
DB Curls	10	8-20		
DB Curls	10	8-20		
DB Curls	10	8-20		
DB Curls	10	8-20		
DB Curls	10	8-20		

Week 10: Volume Training

How did you like Volume Training? Could you complete 10 reps on all 10 sets? It should have been difficult! That's why your body is going to be lean, fit and strong.

A strange phenomenon with this workout occurs around the 6th or 7th set. You become stronger. Really! You think there is no possible way you are going to complete the last few sets. But you will and the last few sets actually become easier than the previous sets.

This is called *short-term neural adaptation*. Your body adapts quickly to the extraordinary stress by tapping into all its reserves to perform the exercise. This equals a better body for you!

Because Volume Training is very intense and taxing on your muscles and ability to recuperate, only use this 2-week routine every three months or longer.

Week 10

- Three workouts.
- Non-consecutive days.
- Split routines.
- 2 exercises per workout.
- 10 sets per exercise.
- Rest only 1 minute between sets.
- Rest up to 10 minutes before starting the second exercise.

If a man does his best,
what else is there?

- General George S. Patton

Week 10: Volume Training
Workout 1
-Chest, Shoulders-

Exercise	Your Goal		Your Set	
	Reps	x Weight	Reps	x Weight
1. Twisting Bench	10	8-20		
Twisting Bench	10	8-20		
Twisting Bench	10	8-20		
Twisting Bench	10	8-20		
Twisting Bench	10	8-20		
Twisting Bench	10	8-20		
Twisting Bench	10	8-20		
Twisting Bench	10	8-20		
Twisting Bench	10	8-20		
Twisting Bench	10	8-20		
2. DB Press	10	8-15		
DB Press	10	8-15		
DB Press	10	8-15		
DB Press	10	8-15		
DB Press	10	8-15		
DB Press	10	8-15		
DB Press	10	8-15		
DB Press	10	8-15		
DB Press	10	8-15		
DB Press	10	8-15		

Week 10: Volume Training
Workout 2
-Legs-

Exercise	Your Goal		Your Set	
	Reps x	Weight	Reps x	Weight
1. BB Squats	10	40-80		
BB Squats	10	40-80		
BB Squats	10	40-80		
BB Squats	10	40-80		
BB Squats	10	40-80		
BB Squats	10	40-80		
BB Squats	10	40-80		
BB Squats	10	40-80		
BB Squats	10	40-80		
BB Squats	10	40-80		
2. Calf Raises*	10	100-200		
Calf Raises	10	100-200		
Calf Raises	10	100-200		
Calf Raises	10	100-200		
Calf Raises	10	100-200		
Calf Raises	10	100-200		
Calf Raises	10	100-200		
Calf Raises	10	100-200		
Calf Raises	10	100-200		
Calf Raises	10	100-200		

*Use heavy weights so your calf muscles fatigue

Week 10: Volume Training
Workout 3
-Back, Biceps-

Exercise	Your Goal		Your Set	
	Reps	x Weight	Reps	x Weight
1. Pullovers	10	15-30		
Pullovers	10	15-30		
Pullovers	10	15-30		
Pullovers	10	15-30		
Pullovers	10	15-30		
Pullovers	10	15-30		
Pullovers	10	15-30		
Pullovers	10	15-30		
Pullovers	10	15-30		
Pullovers	10	15-30		
2. BB Curls	10	20-40		
BB Curls	10	20-40		
BB Curls	10	20-40		
BB Curls	10	20-40		
BB Curls	10	20-40		
BB Curls	10	20-40		
BB Curls	10	20-40		
BB Curls	10	20-40		
BB Curls	10	20-40		
BB Curls	10	20-40		

The first wealth is health.

- Emerson

Week 11: Circuit Training

You are nearing the end of your intense 12-week program. The best way show off your new muscles is to lean out with Circuit Training.

Circuit Training consists of 5 exercises, higher reps and little rest. You set up the 5 exercises, so you can go to each one with little or no rest. By using higher reps (around 15) you combine weight training with a cardiovascular activity. This has an awesome leaning-out effect.

Also, because this is a different type of workout, you will continue to trick your body into adding new muscle and burning fat.

To make Circuit Training even more effective, you are going to change your rep tempo. Over the first 10 weeks, you have been using a nice controlled rep speed. 2-3 seconds lowering the weight and 1-2 seconds lifting the weight. But occasionally changing your rep speed will trigger new progress. This is especially true if you have been lifting weights for more than a year. Changing the speed is another variety technique that will keep you from plateauing!

Instead of a nice slow rep tempo, you will go fast. But in control! Explode on the lifting (positive part) of the exercise. Make sure you slow down and stop before you lock out. Then lower (negative part) the weight to the starting position stopping right before you lock out. Lower the weight quickly, about one second, but in control of the weight.

Week 11: Circuit Training

You should never feel like you have bad form or that you are not in control of the weights. Slow down or lighten up the weights as needed. You are not going super fast, just a faster tempo than normal, especially exploding through the lifting part of the exercise.

Week 11

- Three workouts.
- Non-consecutive days.
- Split routines.
- 5 exercises each circuit.
- Little or no rest between 5 exercises.
- Rest 2-3 minutes before starting next circuit.
- 15 reps to fatigue.
- Fast rep speed.

*As I see it every day
you do one of two things:
build health or produce disease
in yourself.*

- **Adelle Davis**

Week 11: Circuit Training
Workout 1
-Lower Body-

Exercise	Your Goal		Your Set	
	Reps x	Weight	Reps x	Weight
1. Leg Extensions	15	20-40		
Leg Curls	15	25-50		
DB Squats	15	10-20		
Leg Press	15	75-125		
Calf Raises	15	75-125		
2. Leg Extensions	15	20-40		
Leg Curls	15	25-50		
DB Squats	15	10-20		
Leg Press	15	75-125		
Calf Raises	15	75-125		
3. Leg Extensions	15	20-40		
Leg Curls	15	25-50		
DB Squats	15	10-20		
Leg Press	15	75-125		
Calf Raises	15	75-125		

Week 11: Circuit Training
Workout 2
-Upper Body-

Exercise	Your Goal		Your Set	
	Reps x	Weight	Reps x	Weight
1. Incline Curls	15	8-15		
BB Bench Press	15	40-80		
BB Press	15	20-35		
BB Curls	15	20-35		
Kickbacks	15	5-10		
2. Incline Curls	15	8-15		
BB Bench Press	15	40-80		
BB Press	15	20-35		
BB Curls	15	20-35		
Kickbacks	15	5-10		
3. Incline Curls	15	8-15		
BB Bench Press	15	40-80		
BB Press	15	20-35		
BB Curls	15	20-35		
Kickbacks	15	5-10		

Week 11: Circuit Training
Workout 3
-Total Body-

Exercise	Your Goal		Your Set	
	Reps x	Weight	Reps x	Weight
1. Walking Lunges	F	10-30		
DB Squats	10	10-25		
Ball V-Ups	10	0		
DB Bench Press	10	15-30		
2 DB Pullovers	10	5-15		
2. Walking Lunges	F	10-30		
DB Squats	10	10-25		
Ball V-Ups	10	0		
DB Bench Press	10	15-30		
2 DB Pullovers	10	5-15		
3. Walking Lunges	F	10-30		
DB Squats	10	10-25		
Ball V-Ups	10	0		
DB Bench Press	10	15-30		
2 DB Pullovers	10	5-15		
4. Walking Lunges	F	10-30		
DB Squats	10	10-25		
Ball V-Ups	10	0		
DB Bench Press	10	15-30		
2 DB Pullovers	10	5-15		

*I believe that
anyone can conquer fear
by doing the things
he fears to do,
provided he keeps doing
them until he gets
a record of successful
experiences behind him.*

-Eleanor Roosevelt

Week 12: Circuit Training

Week 12 already! How do you look and feel?

Did you...

lose weight?
gain strength?
build muscle?
increase energy?

You should be seeing and feeling all of the above or there is something wrong! Are you showing up and giving your best effort every workout? I know you are because you want to look GREAT!

One more week of the leaning out and bringing out the nice definition in your new body.

Week 12

- Three workouts.
- Non-consecutive days.
- Split routines.
- 5 exercises each circuit.
- Little or no rest between 5 exercises.
- Rest 2-3 minutes before starting next circuit.
- 15 reps to fatigue.
- Fast rep speed.

Week 12: Circuit Training
Workout 1
-Chest, Shoulders, Triceps-

Exercise	Your Goal		Your Set	
	Reps x	Weight	Reps x	Weight
1. Incline Flys	15	10-20		
Incline DB Bench	15	10-20		
BB Press	15	15-30		
Side Raise	15	5-10		
Pushdowns	15	25-40		
2. Incline Flys	15	10-20		
Incline DB Bench	15	10-20		
BB Press	15	15-30		
Side Raise	15	5-10		
Pushdowns	15	25-40		
3. Incline Flys	15	10-20		
Incline DB Bench	15	10-20		
BB Press	15	15-30		
Side Raise	15	5-10		
Pushdowns	15	25-40		

Week 12: Circuit Training
Workout 2
-Abs, Legs-

Exercise	Your Goal Reps x Weight		Your Set Reps x Weight	
1. Rev. Crunches	F	0		
Crunches	15	0		
Leg Curls	15	25-40		
Leg Extensions	15	25-40		
Leg Press	15	75-100		
2. Rev. Crunches	F	0		
Crunches	15	0		
Leg Curls	15	25-40		
Leg Extensions	15	25-40		
Leg Press	15	75-100		
3. Rev. Crunches	F	0		
Crunches	15	0		
Leg Curls	15	25-40		
Leg Extensions	15	25-40		
Leg Press	15	75-100		
4. Rev. Crunches	F	0		
Crunches	15	0		
Leg Curls	15	25-40		
Leg Extensions	15	25-40		
Leg Press	15	75-100		

Week 12: Circuit Training
Workout 3
-Back, Biceps-

Exercise	Your Goal Reps x Weight		Your Set Reps x Weight	
1. 2 DB Pullovers	15	8-15		
Rear Raise	15	3-10		
Incline Curls	15	8-15		
Hammer Curls	15	8-15		
Lat Pulldown*	15	40-70		
2. 2 DB Pullovers	15	8-15		
Rear Raise	15	3-10		
Incline Curls	15	8-15		
Hammer Curls	15	8-15		
Lat Pulldown*	15	40-70		
3. 2 DB Pullovers	15	8-15		
Rear Raise	15	3-10		
Incline Curls	15	8-15		
Hammer Curls	15	8-15		
Lat Pulldown*	15	40-70		

*Use the Triangle Bar

Sickness is felt,
but health not at all.

- Thomas Fuller, M.D.

Now What Should I Do?

After completing the 12-week program you should be seeing and feeling amazing transformations in your body. Keep it up! Now the best thing to do is <u>start the program over again</u>. You will be stronger, more fit, your body fat will be reduced and you will be ready to make even greater progress!

Start the program over knowing you are going to be stronger, so you are going to attempt lifting more weight. Increasing the weight just a small amount can make big differences in your fitness results.

If you find some exercises that personally work better for you, replace them with the exercises you do not like. Just remember not to get stuck in a rut of using the same exercises or workouts too often. Your results will diminish if you do not use variety.

Keep up the outstanding work!

> Please keep me informed on your progress and questions.
> **james@weighttrainingworkouts.com**

"Done correctly, weight training is the most efficient, effective, and safest form of exercise there is, and it won't be long before people realize it."

-Dr Worthy, American College of Sports Medicine

To follow,
without halt,
one aim:
There's the secret of success.

- Anna Pavlova

Part II
The Best Weight Training Exercises

Basic Muscle Chart

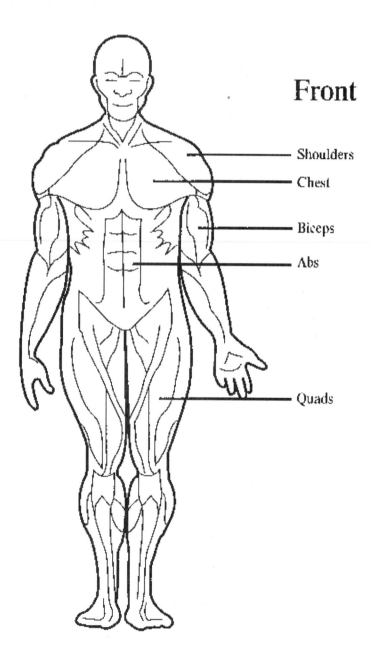

Front

— Shoulders

— Chest

— Biceps

— Abs

— Quads

Basic Muscle Chart

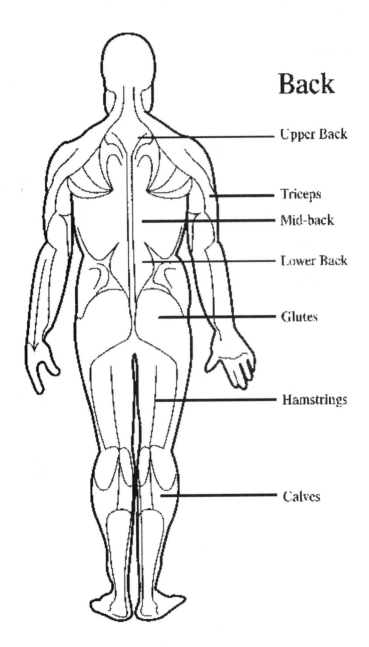

Back

- Upper Back
- Triceps
- Mid-back
- Lower Back
- Glutes
- Hamstrings
- Calves

Abs

Ab Bench Crunches

Muscles Used: Abs
Starting Weight: 0-10

- Set or use a bench with 10-30 degree decline.
- Lock-in legs.
- Place hands across chest.
- Do not put your hands behind your head, you can pull on your neck and spine.
- Slowly lower your body, keeping your back slightly rounded.
- Lower upper body until nearing parallel to the floor.
  Do not go too low until you are strong enough!
- Keep abs tight throughout movement.
- Return to starting position, stopping just before you are straight up to keep tension on the abs.
- Repeat until set is complete.

Abs

Ab Bench Crunches

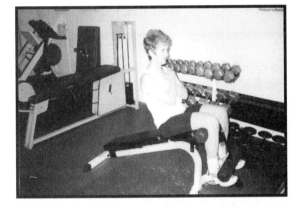

Abs

Ball Crunches

Muscles Used: Abs
Starting Weight: 0-10

- Lie on the ball with your knees bent at about a 90-degree angle. Make sure your feet are securely on the floor, wide enough to stabilize your upper body.
- *Make sure you are careful the first few times you perform ball crunches. You could be unstable and roll off the ball, so do not have any equipment around you that could be potentially dangerous.*
- Put your hands across your chest.
- Slowly curl up keeping your abs tight.
- Exhale as you curl up.
- Curl up about 30 degrees.
- Slowly lower until you feel a nice stretch in your abs.
- Inhale as you lower.
- Repeat until set is complete.
- Only lower as far as you feel comfortable. *Make sure you do not go too far back until your abs and lower back are strong enough!* The ball works super for abs because you can lower past parallel to the floor. Your abs work approximately 30 degrees forward <u>and</u> 30 degrees backwards. When you perform all your ab exercises on a flat surface, you are only doing half the range of motion. The ball helps you train the abs through their full range.
- TIP: Add a weight plate or dumbbell across your chest when you need more resistance.

Ball Crunches

Abs

Ball V-Ups

Muscles Used: Lower Abs, Upper Abs
Starting Weight: 0 lbs.

- Lie on the floor placing the ball between your knees and lower legs. Hands across you chest.
- Slowly lift up your upper body <u>and</u> legs at the same time.
- Exhale as you lift.
- Lift you upper body about 30 degrees while pulling your legs toward your chest area, squeezing your abs tight.
- Pause on the top position.
- Slowly lower to starting position.
- Inhale while lowering.
- Stop right before your shoulders and feet touch the floor.
- This keeps constant tension on your abs.
- Repeat until set is complete.
- TIP: If the exercise is too hard to perform or you become fatigued quickly, keep your upper body on the floor and just curl up your legs. Concentrate on you lower abs doing the work.

Abs

Ball V-Ups

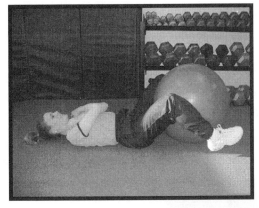

Abs

Crunches

Muscles Used: Abs
Starting Weight: 0-10

- Lie on your back.
- Knees bent, feet on the floor.
- Put hands across your chest.
  Do not put your hands behind your head.
- Curl up about 30-degrees. Do not go up all the way.
- Hold for a second.
- Slowly lower until right before your shoulders fully touch the floor. This will keep tension on your abs.
- Repeat until set is complete.
- TIP: Keep your stomach flexed during the entire exercise- *"like you are getting ready for someone to punch you in the stomach."*
- TIP: When adding weight for resistance, hold a weight plate or a dumbbell across your chest.

Crunches

Abs

Reverse Crunches

Muscles Used: Lower Abs
Starting Weight: 0

- Set bench at approximately a 30-degree decline.
- Lay on your back, head at the top of the bench. Make sure your head is flat on the bench.
- Hang on to the top of the bench. This can be the hardest part of the exercise in the beginning. Just grab onto whatever you can, it will become easier.
- Curl up your legs as far as you feel comfortable, knees bent.
- Pause for a second at the top.
- Slowly lower legs.
- Lower as far as you feel comfortable. Your lower back and abs will become stronger with this exercise.
- Repeat until set is complete.
- TIP: Use a spotter to help lift your legs.
- TIP: If your lower back is weak, substitute another ab exercise until you feel strong enough to perform reverse crunches.

Reverse Crunches

Abs

Wood Chop

Muscles Used: Abs, Entire Mid-Section
Starting Weight: 10-20 lbs.

- Use the rope attachment on a low pulley.
- Stand with you with feet shoulder width apart or wider so you have stability.
- Make sure you are far enough away from the pulley, 1 to 2 feet, so you can perform the exercise through the full range of motion.
- Grasp both ends of the rope together, with your palms facing down.
- With your arms slightly bent, pull up rope diagonally and twist body at the same time.
- *Concentrate on your mid-section pulling the weight up, not your arms.*
- Exhale when pulling up.
- Stop when you are fully extended.
- Slowly lower the weight, keeping your mid-section tight all the way to the starting position.
- Inhale while lowering the weight.
- Repeat until set is complete.
- TIP: This is a very mental exercise! You have to think about your entire midsection doing the work, not your arms.
- TIP: Remember to turn around and do your other side.

Wood Chop

Back

Lat Pulldown - Wide Grip

Muscles Used: Upper & Mid Back, Biceps
Starting Weight: 40-70 lbs.

- Grasp the straight bar with an overhand grip, palms facing away from you.
- Hands 2-3 inches wider than your shoulders. Do not go too wide, this can put undue stress on your shoulders.
- Holding bar, sit down and lock knees under pad. Adjust height of pad if needed.
- *Lean back, with chest out during entire movement.*
- First movement should be pulling your shoulder blades back and together. *Think of someone putting a finger between your shoulder blades and you trying to squeeze their finger.*
- Pull the bar all the way down to the mid-upper chest area, concentrating on your upper back.
- Elbows half way between your sides and straight out.
- Stop for a second, then slowly resist the bar all the way up. Remember to keep your chest out and shoulders back through the entire movement.
- Keep back muscles tight.
- Return the bar all the way up until you feel a slight stretch in your mid-upper back muscles.
- Repeat until set is complete.

Back

Lat Pulldown - Wide Grip

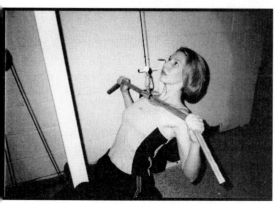

115

Back

Lat Pulldown – Underhand Grip

Muscles Used: Mid Back, Biceps
Starting Weight: 40-70 lbs.

Same as Lat Pulldown - Wide Grip except:

- Underhand grip with palms facing you.
- Hands approximately 1 –2 feet apart.
- Pull to low-mid chest area.
- Elbows along the sides of your body.

Lat Pulldown – Underhand Grip

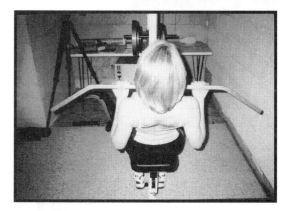

Back

Lat Pulldown - Triangle Bar

Muscles Used: Mid-Outer Back, Biceps
Starting Weight: 40-70 lbs.

Same as Lat Pulldown - Wide Grip except:
- Use the Triangle Bar (also called the V-Bar).
- Palms facing each other.
- Pull to mid-chest.
- Elbows along the sides of your body.
- Concentrate on mid and outer sides of back.

Triangle Bar

Lat Pulldown - Triangle Bar

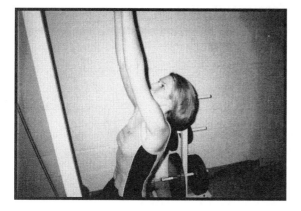

Back

Dumbbell Pullovers

Muscles Used: Back, Triceps, Chest
Starting Weight: 15-25 lbs.

- Lay on the bench with your feet on the floor or bench.
- Your head at the end of the bench. Make sure your head is supported on the bench.
- Grasp a dumbbell on the inside end with your palms flat, overlapping each other securely. See illustration below.
- Keep elbows in and pointed forward, towards your feet.
- Slowly lower the dumbbell behind your head
- Keep your muscles tight!
- Lower until upper arms are beside your head and lower arms are bent.
- Feel a good stretch in your abs, back and triceps. Do not go too far down right away. If your shoulders start to feel weak, stop. You will become stronger and more flexible.
- <u>Slowly pull up with your elbows, not your hands.</u> This will emphasize your back muscles.
- Straighten your arms towards the top of movement.
- Stop when the dumbbell is straight over your chest/shoulder area.
- Repeat until set is complete.

Dumbbell Pullovers

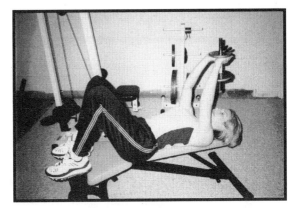

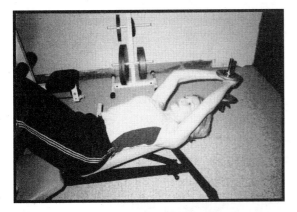

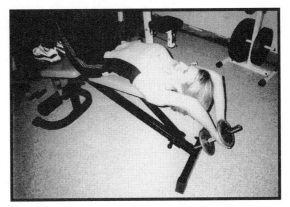

Back

2 Dumbbell Pullovers

Muscles Used: Back, Triceps, Chest
Starting Weight: 5-15 lbs.

- Lay on the bench with your feet on the floor or the bench.
- Your head at the end of the bench. Make sure your head is supported on the bench.
- Grasp 2 dumbbells. Hold straight up over your shoulder area.
- Palms facing each other.
- Keep elbows in and pointed forward, towards your feet.
- Slowly lower the dumbbells behind your head.
- Keep your muscles tight!
- Lower until upper arms are beside your head and lower arms are bent.
- Feel a good stretch in your abs, back and triceps.
- Do not go too far down right away. If your shoulders start to feel weak, stop. You will become stronger and more flexible.
- Slowly pull up with your elbows, not your hands. This will emphasize your back muscles.
- Straighten your arms towards the top of movement.
- Stop when the dumbbells is straight over your chest/shoulder area.
- Repeat until set is complete.

2 Dumbbell Pullovers

Back

2 Dumbbell Rows

Muscles Used: Mid Back, Upper and Lower Back, Biceps
Starting Weight: 10-20 lbs.

- Sit on the end of a bench.
- Feet close together.
- Grasp 2 dumbbells.
- Bend over keeping your back flat and your head up.
- *Make sure to keep your head up or in the neutral position during the entire exercise. This will keep your back flat. If you look down your back will start to round, which will put undue stress on your lower back.*
- Keeping head up and chest out, pull up dumbbells squeezing your shoulder blades together.
- Keep your elbows in, pulling along sides of your body.
- Exhale as you pull up the dumbbells.
- Squeeze you shoulder blades together on the top, feeling your back do the work.
- Slowly lower the weight, keeping your head up and back flat.
- Inhale on the lowering phase.
- TIP: Move your upper body with the motion. When your pulling the weight up, move your upper body up with the weight stopping at about a 70 degree angle to the floor. When lowering the weight, lower your upper body with the weight. This will help keep stress off your lower back.

2 Dumbbell Rows

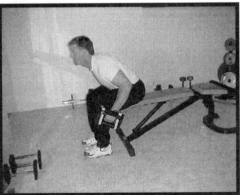

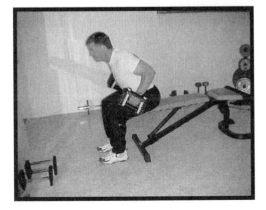

Biceps

Barbell Curls

Muscles Used: Biceps
Starting Weight: 20-30 lbs.

- Standing, feet shoulder width apart.
- Knees slightly bent.
- Palms forward, slightly wider than shoulder width apart.
- Elbows touching your sides.
- Curl the weight up towards your shoulders/chin area until biceps are fully contracted.
- Look straight ahead and do not to arch your back during lifting phase.
- Slowly lower the weight.
- Stop right before your elbows lock out.
- Repeat until set is complete.

Biceps

Barbell Curls

Biceps

Cable Curls

Muscles Used: Biceps
Starting Weight: 15-30 lbs.

- Stand facing the low pulley machine.
- 1-2 feet away from the pulley.
- Grasp bar, palms up, about shoulder width apart.
- You can also use the rope attachment. Your palms will be facing each when using the rope.
- Keep your elbows *stuck* at your sides during entire movement.
- Curl up weight concentrating on your biceps doing the work.
- Keep your back straight.
- Exhale as you lift the weight.
- Slowly lower the weight to starting position, letting the biceps do all the work.
- Stop right before your elbows lock out. This will keep constant tension on you biceps and is easy on your joints.
- Inhale as you lower the weight.
- Repeat until set is complete.

Biceps
Cable Curls

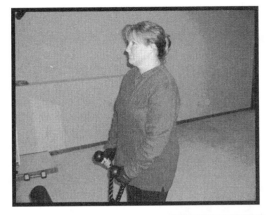

Biceps

Dumbbell Curls

Muscles Used: Biceps
Starting Weight: 10-20 lbs.

- Seated, feet firmly on the floor.
- Back straight.
- Dumbbells hanging at your sides.
- Palms facing each other.
- Elbows pressed against your sides (elbows do not move).
- Curl dumbbells at the same time towards your shoulders, rotating palms so they are facing up when biceps are fully contracted.
- Slowly lower weight, rotating palms back so they are facing each other again at the bottom.
- Stop right before elbows lock out.
- Repeat until set is complete.

130

Biceps

Dumbbell Curls

131

Biceps

Hammer Curls

Muscles Used: Outer Biceps
Starting Weight: 8-15 lbs.

- Seated, feet firmly on the floor.
- Back straight.
- Dumbbells hanging at your sides.
- Palms facing each other.
- Elbows pressed against your sides.
- Elbows do not move during entire movement.
- Curl dumbbells at the same time towards your shoulders, keeping your palms facing each other.
- Exhale as you lift the weight.
- Slowly lower weight to starting position.
- Stop right before elbows lock out.
- Inhale as you lower the weight.
- Repeat until set is complete.

Hammer Curls

Biceps

Incline Curls

Muscles Used: Lower Biceps
Starting Weight: 8-15 lbs.

- <u>Set or use a bench at a 70-80 degree angle.</u>
- Seated, feet firmly on the floor or locked in place.
- Back flat against the bench.
- You can keep your head up (off the bench) if it is more comfortable.
- Dumbbells hanging at your sides.
- Palms facing each other.
- Elbows pressed against your sides.
- Elbows do not move during entire movement.
- Curl dumbbells at the same time towards your shoulders, turning you palms up during the movement.
- Exhale as you lift the weight.
- Slowly lower weight to starting position.
- Turning your palms back to facing each other.
- Stop right before elbows lock out.
- Inhale as you lower the weight.
- Repeat until set is complete.
- TIP: When your biceps become fatigued, you can keep your palms up the entire movement. This should help you complete a couple extra reps.

Biceps

Incline Curls

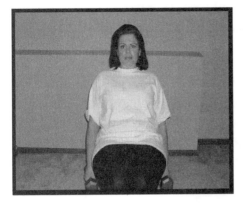

Chest

Barbell Bench Press

Muscles Used: Chest, Shoulders, Triceps
Starting Weight: 30-60 lbs.

- Lay flat on the bench with your feet on the floor or bench, keeping your lower back flat.
- Grasp barbell, palms facing forward, slightly wider than shoulder width apart. You can experiment with your hand position but do not go too wide or narrow because this can put undue stress on your shoulders.
- Slowly lower the bar to your mid-chest with elbows straight out to the sides.
- Lightly touch middle of the chest. Do not bounce! Upper and lower arms should be at a right angle.
- Feel a stretch in your chest and mentally push up with your chest muscles.
- Stop right before you lock out on top.
- Repeat until set is complete.
- TIP: Make sure to use a spotter with heavy weights.

Barbell Bench Press

Chest

Dumbbell Bench Press

Muscles Used: Chest, Shoulders, Triceps
Starting Weight: 10-20 lbs.

- Lay flat on the bench with your feet on the floor or bench, keeping your lower back flat.
- Bring dumbbells to the starting position with your palms facing forward towards your feet.
- Slowly lower dumbbells, elbows straight out to the sides.
- Lower until you feel a good stretch in your chest and your arms are at about a 90-degree angle.
- If your front shoulders start to pull too much, stop.
  You will become stronger and more flexible with practice.
- Push straight up.
- Stop right before you lock out on top.
- Repeat until set is complete.

Dumbbell Bench Press

Chest

Incline Dumbbell Bench Press

Muscles Used: Upper Chest, Shoulders, Triceps
Starting Weight: 8-20 lbs.

- Set or use a bench with approximately a 45-degree incline.
- Feet on floor and lower back pushed against the backrest.
- Bring dumbbells to the starting position with your palms facing forward towards your feet.
- Slowly lower dumbbells, elbows straight out to the sides.
- Lower until you feel a good stretch in your upper chest and your arms are at about a 90-degree angle. If your front shoulders start to pull too much, stop.
- *You will become stronger and more flexible with practice.*
- Push straight up.
- Stop right before your elbows lock out on top.
- Repeat until set is complete.

Chest

Incline Dumbbell Bench Press

Chest

Incline Flys

Muscles Used: Upper Chest
Starting Weight: 8-15 lbs.

- Lie on an incline bench, feet on the floor.
- Bench should be about a 45-degree angle.
- Bring the dumbbells to the starting position.
- Palms facing forward.
- *Keep elbows slightly bent during the movement.*
- Slowly lower dumbbells straight out to your sides.
- *Let gravity pull the weight down.*
- Keep your chest muscles tight.
- Lower until you feel a stretch in your chest muscles.
- Make sure you stop lowering the weight if you start to feel your front shoulders pulling too much.
- *Mentally pull up with your chest, not concentrating on your arms.*
- Keep chest flexed throughout movement, especially the top part of the exercise.
- Repeat until set is complete.
- TIP: The movement should be in an arc, with gravity pulling the dumbbells down. Keep your arms about the same angle throughout the movement, this is not a pressing movement.

142

Incline Flys

Chest

Twisting Dumbbell Bench Press

Muscles Used: Chest, Shoulders, Triceps
Starting Weight: 10-20 lbs.

- Grasp dumbbells and lie on a flat bench.
- Feet on the floor or bench, back flat.
- Start at the bottom position with your palms facing each other.
- *Push the dumbbells up, at the same time pushing your elbows back and up, turning your palms forward so they are facing your feet.*
- Stop right before your elbows lock out.
- Exhale as you lift the weight.
- Slowly lower the weight to starting position, turning your palms in and pulling your elbows in at the same time.
- Inhale as you lower the weight.
- Repeat until set is complete.
- TIP: Concentrate on your chest muscles during the entire exercise, not your arms.
- TIP: Practice with light weights until you feel comfortable with the exercise <u>and</u> can feel you chest doing the work. This exercise may take a little time to perfect the form and feeling your chest do all the work.

144

Twisting Dumbbell Bench Press

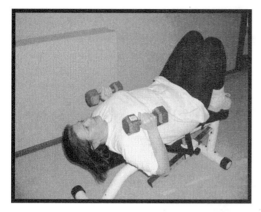

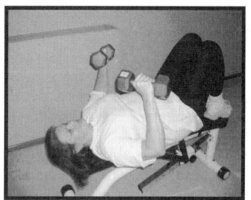

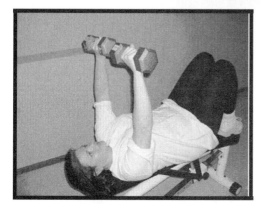

Legs

Barbell Squats

Muscles Used: Quads, Glutes, Hamstrings
Starting Weight: 45-75 lbs.

- Tip - Use a squat rack or a spotter if available.
- Place barbell on your upper back, not on your neck. Use a bar pad if available.
- Feet shoulder width apart, toes slightly pointed out about 10 degrees.
- Focus eyes straight ahead during entire movement.
- Slowly lower, bending at the knees. Think of sitting down in a chair.
- Your hips and butt go back. Knees straight over your feet.
- Knees behind your feet. If your knees are going in front of your feet too much, it puts undue stress on your knees. Make sure your rear end is going out.
- Keep your back straight. Your back will be *flat* but at a 70-80 degree angle to the floor.
- Stop when your quads become parallel to the floor. This is your goal, but start by only lowering a <u>short distance</u> until you learn the exercise and become stronger.
- Push straight up under control.
- Breath out when you are half way up in the return phase.
- Stop right before your knees lock out.
- Repeat until set is complete.
- TIP: If your lower back starts to develop a dull throb, stop and rest. Your lower back will probably be the first muscles to become tired, but will become stronger with practice.

Barbell Squats

Legs

Dumbbell Squats

Muscles Used: Quads, Glutes, Hamstrings
Starting Weight: 10-20lbs.

- Grasp dumbbells, palms facing each other at your sides.
- Feet shoulder width apart or a little narrower so the dumbbells do not get in the way. Toes slightly pointed out 10 degrees.
- Focus eyes straight ahead during entire movement.
- Slowly lower, bending at the knees. Think of sitting in a chair.
- Your hips and butt go back. Knees straight over your feet.
- Knees behind your feet. If your knees are going in front of your feet too much, it puts undue stress on your knees. Make sure your rear end is going out.
- Keep your back straight. Your back will be *flat* but will be at a 70-80 degree angle to the floor.
- Stop when your quads become parallel to the floor..
- Push straight up under control.
- Breath out when you are half way up in the return phase.
- Stop right before your knees lock out.
- Repeat until set is complete.
- TIP: If your heels start to lift up while lowering, use small weight plates, 5 or 10 lbs. under your heels to help stabilize your body.

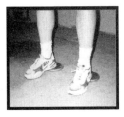

Dumbbell Squats

Legs

Deadlifts

Muscles Used: Hamstrings, Glutes, Lower Back
Starting Weight: 20-45 lbs.

- Grasp barbell, palms facing you.
- Hands shoulder width apart.
- Feet straight-ahead, about a foot apart.
- Hold barbell with arms straight, at mid thigh.
- Keep back flat, shoulders back, chest out and knees slightly bent throughout movement.
- Lower bar, right in front of your body, until about mid-shin level. *Do not go too far down, only until it feels comfortable.*
- Hips and rear end go back, bending at the waist.
- Feel a stretch in your hamstrings.
- Pull up to the starting position.
- <u>Concentrate on your hamstrings</u>, not your back.
- Repeat until set is complete.
- TIP: Remember to keep your back flat. Do not round your back. Keep your head in the neutral position.
- TIP: <u>Do not use too heavy of weights.</u>

Legs

Calf Raises

Muscles Used: Calf
Starting Weight: 75-100 lbs.

- Do calf raises on the Leg Press Machine.
- Place balls of feet on the edge of the platform, knees relatively straight.
- Push up as far as possible until you feel a stretch at the top of the movement.
- Slowly lower heels until you feel a good stretch in your calves.
- Repeat until set is complete.
- TIP: If you don't have access to the Leg Press, you can do calf raises on the stairs, a calf block or any calf machine. There are many excellent types of machines at health clubs and gyms. Use the same form on all calf exercises.

Calf Raises

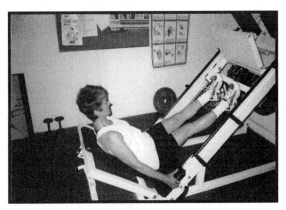

Legs

Leg Extensions

Muscles Used: Quads
Starting Weight: 30-50 lbs.

- Sit on the Leg Extension machine.
- Back firmly against the back pad.
- Back of knee against pad. Adjust the machine if needed.
- Lower leg pad on lower shin. Adjust the machine if needed.
- Slowly raise the weight until thigh is fully flexed and hold for a second, feeling your quads flex.
- *Do not hyperextend knees by raising the weight too fast.*
- Slowly lower.
- Stop before your lower leg goes past a 90-degree angle. By doing this, it keeps undue pressure off your knees.
- Repeat set until complete.

154

Leg Extensions

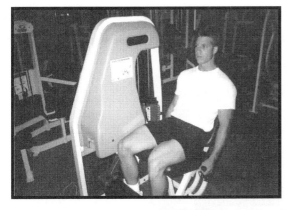

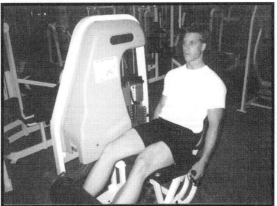

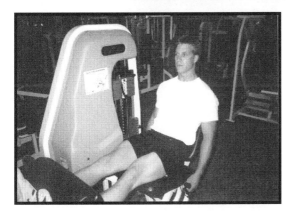

Legs

Leg Curls

Muscles Used: Hamstrings
Starting Weight: 30-50 lbs.

- Lie face down on the Leg Curl machine.
- Knees right behind the thigh pad.
- Lower leg pad above your heels.
- Grab handles or the bench.
- Pull the weight up slowly, especially the first 2-3 inches. This will make the hamstrings do the work.
- Stop when your feet are straight up or close to your rear end.
- *Keep your hips in contact with the bench at all times.*
- Slowly lower the weight.
- Stop right before your knees lock out.
- Repeat until set is complete.

Leg Curls

Legs

Leg Press

Muscles Used: Quads, Hamstrings, Glutes
Starting Weight: 75-125 lbs.

- Adjust the backrest so it is near the middle setting.
- Higher up if you are small person, lower if you are larger.
- Back and glutes firmly against the pads.
- Place your feet on the top half of the platform.
- Feet shoulder width apart.
- Toes *slightly* pointed out about 10-degrees.
- Grasp handles, push up platform and unlock weights.
- Slowly lower knees towards your chest.
- When your legs go slightly past 90-degrees, stop. Make sure your butt does not start to lift up. If it does, stop, you have gone too far. That can put undue stress on your back.
- Slowly push the weights up, through your heels. This will take pressure off your knees.
- Stop right before your knees lock out.
- Repeat until set is complete.
- TIP: Find out how much the Leg Press weighs before you add weight. Every machine is different.
- TIP: Verticle and Horizontal Leg Press machines also work well. Use the same form as above.

Legs

Leg Press

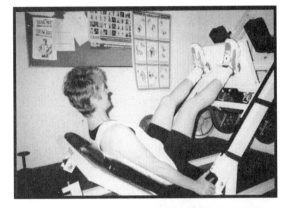

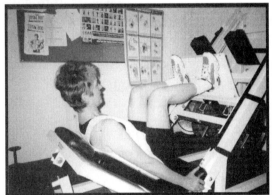

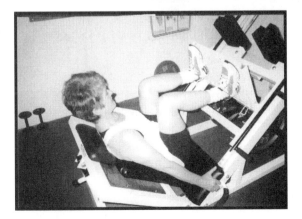

159

Legs

Stationary Lunges

Muscles Used: Glutes, Hamstrings, Quads
Starting Weight: 0 Lbs

- You exercise one leg at a time.
- Grasp a bench, machine, etc., something stable.
- Step forward with lead leg.
- Slowly lower straight down, keeping your back flat.
- Do not lean forward.
- Bend knee of lead leg until it reaches close to 90-degree angle. In the beginning, only bend your front knee as far as you feel comfortable.
- Keep knee over and behind lead foot. Make sure you are going straight up and down. Do <u>not</u> lean forward.
- Knee of back leg should be a few inches off the floor.
- Push straight up.
- Stop right before your front knee locks out.
- Repeat until set is complete.
- Switch lead leg.
- TIP: When you become stronger you can do lunges without holding on to a stable object. After that becomes too easy, you can add dumbbells in each hand for more resistance.

160

Legs

Stationary Lunges

Legs

Walking Lunges

Muscles Used: Glutes, Hamstrings, Quads
Starting Weight: 5-15 lbs.

- Grasp dumbbells.
- Stand straight up with the dumbbells hanging at your sides.
- Feet hip-width width apart and toes pointed straight ahead.
- Take a step forward. *Make sure you step forward easy, don't come down hard on your front foot.*
- Keep your upper body upright and head looking straight ahead.
- Bend your lead leg so your upper leg is parallel to the ground.
- *Keep your lead knee directly over your foot when lowering. Do not lean forward and let your knee drift in front of your foot. This is hard on your knees.*
- Inhale as you lower.
- Push up while bring your back leg goes forward, just like you are walking.
- Exhale as you push up.
- Take a step forward. *Make sure you step forward easy, don't come down hard on your front foot.*
- Repeat until your legs are fatigued.
- TIP: If you ever start to lose your balance, STOP! Walking Lunges are a great exercise but require perfect form for safety.
- TIP: If you are new to lunges, make sure you start with Stationary Lunges until you feel comfortable. Then start using Walking Lunges with very light weights!

162

Legs

Walking Lunges

Shoulders

Barbell Press

Muscles Used: Shoulders, Triceps, Upper Back
Starting Weight: 20-40 lbs.

- Stand with feet shoulder width apart.
- Keep knees slightly bent.
- Bring barbell to the starting position.
- Palms forward, just slightly wider than shoulder width apart.
- Push barbell straight up in front of your face.
- Be sure to look straight ahead during entire movement, this will keep your back as straight as possible.
- Stop right before elbows lock out.
- *Slowly lower barbell to chin/neck level.*
- Keeps tension on your shoulders.
- Repeat until set is complete.
- TIP: Use a spotter if available.

Shoulders

Barbell Press

Shoulders

Dumbbell Press

Muscles Used: Shoulders, Triceps
Starting Weight: 8-15 lbs.

- Seated, back flat against bench, feet firmly on the floor.
- Grasp dumbbells.
- Bring dumbbells to starting position, palms facing forward.
- Arms should be at a right angle.
- Push straight up, stopping right before your elbows lock out.
- Make sure to keep your back straight. Keep it pressed against the backrest.
- Slowly lower.
- Stop when dumbbells are in line with your ears, arms at a right angle. It keeps tension on your shoulders.
- Repeat until set is complete.

Shoulders

Dumbbell Press

Shoulders

Front Raise

Muscles Used: Front Shoulders, Upper Back
Starting Weight: 3-10 lbs.

- Stand with your feet shoulder width apart or a little wider.
- Grasp 2 dumbbells with your palms facing you.
- Keep your elbows slightly bent during the entire movement.
- Raise the dumbbells directly in front of you.
- Raise to head level.
- Exhale as you lift the dumbbells.
- Keep your back flat. Don't arch your back.
- *Concentrate on your shoulders and upper back lifting the weights, not your arms.*
- Slowly lower the dumbbells, stopping before the weights are all the way down. This will keep constant tension on the muscles.
- Inhale as you lower.
- Repeat until set is complete.

Front Raise

Shoulders

Rear Raise

Muscles Used: Rear Shoulders, Upper Back
Starting Weight: 3-10 lbs.

- Sit on the end of a flat bench.
- Feet close together.
- Grasp 2 dumbbells, palms facing each other.
- Bend over, keeping your back flat and your head up.
- *Try to look forward during entire movement. This will keep your back flat. You do not want it to round. This will happen if you start to look down, putting your back in an unsafe position.*
- Keeping your elbows slightly bent, raise your arms straight out to the sides like you are flying.
- The dumbbells should be in line with your head.
- Raise the weights as high as you can.
- Squeezing your shoulder blades together.
- Exhale as you lift the dumbbells.
- Pause on the top.
- SLOWLY lower the weights, feeling your rear shoulders and back doing the work.
- Inhale as you lower.
- Repeat until set is complete.

Rear Raise

Shoulders

Side Raise

Muscles Used: Outer Shoulders
Starting Weight: 5-15 lbs.

- Standing.
- Dumbbells at your sides and palms facing each other.
- Keep elbows bent during the entire movement.
- Raise the dumbbells out to the sides like you are flying.
- Stop when the DBs are in line with or slightly above your head.
- Slowly lower, keeping elbows bent.
- Repeat until set is complete.

172

Side Raise

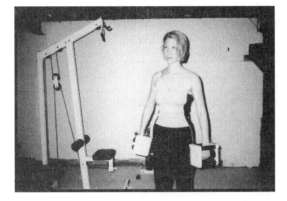

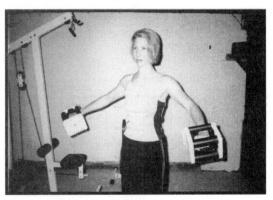

Triceps

Kickbacks

Muscles Used: Triceps
Starting Weight: 3-10 lbs.

- Grasp 2 dumbbells.
- Standing, feet shoulder width apart.
- Bend over, keeping your back flat and your head up.
- Palms facing each other.
- Bring your elbows to your sides.
- *Elbows do not move during the entire exercise.*
- Arms bent at about a 90-degree angle.
- Push the dumbbells back and up, straightening your arms.
- Pause for a second.
- FEEL your triceps flex hard at the top position.
- Exhale.
- Slowly lower to starting position keeping you head up.
- Inhale while lowering.
- Repeat until set is complete.
- TIP: To make kickbacks more effective, only lower the dumbbells about half way and then push back up. You can do this until your triceps start to fatigue and then use full range of motion on the last few reps.

Triceps
Kickbacks

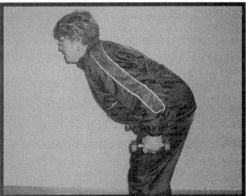

Triceps

Overhead Extensions

Muscles Used: Triceps
Starting Weight: 10-20 lbs.

- Seated, feet firmly on the floor.
- Grasp a dumbbell on the inside end with your palms flat, <u>overlapping each other securely</u>.
- Bring dumbbell to starting position, directly over your head.
- Elbows stay in the same position during the entire movement.
- Slowly lower the weight behind your head.
- *Keep your head up and back straight.*
- Lower as far as possible, feeling a good stretch in your triceps.
- Inhale as you lower.
- Make sure your elbows don't move.
- Push the dumbbells back up to the starting position.
- Stop right before your elbows lock out.
- Exhale as you lift the weight.
- Repeat until your set is complete.

Overhead Extensions

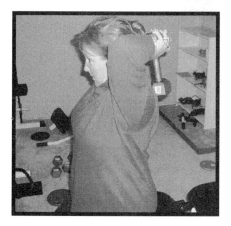

Triceps

Pushdowns

Muscles Used: Triceps
Starting Weight: 25-40 lbs.

- Stand, facing the pulldown machine, about a foot away.
- Keep your back straight, knees slightly bent and feet shoulder width apart.
- Grasp bar, palms facing down, about a foot apart.
- Pull the bar down so your elbows are touching your sides. *Then your elbows will not move during the exercise.*
- Push straight down until arms are straight.
- You should feel your triceps contract.
- Slowly resist weight until about chest height.
- Remember your elbows do not move.
- Repeat until set is complete.
- TIP: You can also use the rope attachment.

Pushdowns

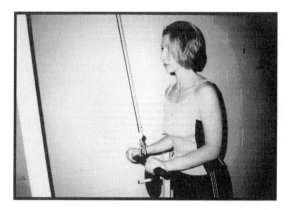

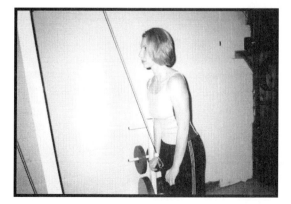

Triceps

SkullKrushers

Muscles Used: Triceps
Starting Weight: 5-15 lbs.

- Grasp 2 dumbbells.
- Lie on a bench.
- Feet firmly on the floor or bench.
- Start with the dumbbells straight over your shoulders.
- Arms straight and elbows pointed towards your feet.
- Palms facing each other.
- Elbows stay in the same position throughout exercise.
- Slowly lower the dumbbells along the sides of your head.
- Lower until you feel a good stretch in your triceps.
- Inhale as you lower.
- Pause at the bottom.
- Return to starting position.
- Stop right before your elbows lock out.
- Exhale as you lift the weights.
- Repeat until set is complete.
- TIP: Be careful not to use too heavy of dumbbells so you can control them around your head!

Triceps

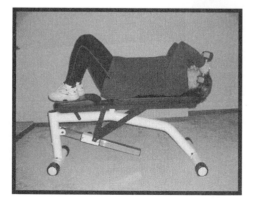

Even More Results!

Looking for more results? I highly recommend following this 12-week program again for added benefits! Many times the second time through a weight training program you will have even better success because you can perform the exercises more efficiently. This means you will be able to do more reps and use more weight...and this equals a better body for you!

Want to download new workouts?
www.weighttrainingworkouts.com

Questions? Comments?
james@weighttrainingworkouts.com

On-line orders for Volume I or II!
www.weighttrainingworkouts.com

Book postal orders!
Volume I - $14.95 or Volume II - $17.95
ALWAYS FREE SHIPPING! (MN add 6.5% tax)
Send Check or Money Order:
Ideal Publishing
33806 Pine View Lane
Crosslake, MN 56442

About the Author

James Orvis is a certified personal trainer and author. Personal training in private residences, health clubs, gyms, senior centers and corporate settings he has developed a simple method for maximum results: The best weight training workouts and exercises in one portable book. James resides in Crosslake, Minnesota with his wife Traci and daughter Maya.

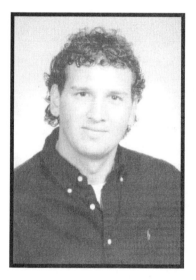

Quick Exercise Finder